W9-AZI-655

Loving Discipline

by
Robert S. McGee

*A Practical Guide To Establishing
Systematic Discipline In Your Home !*

Copyright 1989 © Robert S. McGee

Published by

Rapha
PUBLISHING

HOUSTON, TEXAS

CONTENTS

INTRODUCTION

This booklet was written to instruct parents how to discipline their children in a way that effectively produces both obedience and healthy self-esteem.

There are many good books on the subject. Two that I recommend highly are Charles Swindoll's *Know Your Child* and James Dobson's *Dare To Discipline*. However, in all of my reading, I have found nothing that provides the practical step-by-step approach that parents desperately need.

Unfortunately, our society has moved away from a healthy, Biblical approach to discipline and is polarized so that permissiveness and neglect or anger and abuse are growing as the most widely-used methods of controlling children. In fact, differing views on discipline are a new source of conflict between husbands and wives today. We need to have a fundamental understanding of the principles and goals of discipline so that spouses can agree with one another and form a supportive team to lead the family instead of isolating one another and the children by disagreement, distrust, anger and withdrawal.

The principles offered in this book have helped many parents form a plan for discipline so that their children grow to be mature, responsible adults. The ability to resolve conflict is a key ingredient for a home where parents and children love and encourage each other.

These principles work because they are based on the truths of the Scriptures. You can experience success in disciplining your children. In fact, I've never seen these principles fail when they have been used correctly.

THE NEED FOR DISCIPLINE

The first time I became involved in helping a child with a discipline problem was with a seven-year-old who threw a terrible tantrum when he had to go to school. He yelled and screamed and even bit and clawed his mother. She was told to put him in a school for emotionally disturbed children or in a mental hospital.

Instead of putting him in a mental ward, I told her to make a contract with Johnny. She was going to tell him that he was going to go to school no matter what happened, and he would get three spanks with a ping pong paddle each time he threw a tantrum. Also, they were going to get up thirty minutes earlier every day until he quit the unacceptable behavior to give him time to go through his routine and still be at school on time.

After only two days he was going to school peacefully, and after two weeks he was riding his bike to school. The certainty of the discipline made the fuss unprofitable to the child and the tantrums ceased.

To discipline children properly and consistently, we need to understand the purposes of discipline. There are two primary purposes: to warn and to teach. Discipline is an effective warning that the child's behavior is harmful to himself or harmful to others. It demonstrates that there are awful consequences to misbehavior, usually much worse than the pain of the discipline itself. (For example: discipline for running out in the street without looking for cars.)

The second purpose for discipline is to teach the child appropriate behavior. The goals of teaching and correction fall into four main areas:

1. Correct response to authority.
2. Self-control.
3. Love.

> Love is strong and active. Some of us think that love is always warm and fun while discipline is harsh and bitter, but discipline is (or can be) an act of love to protect and teach the child. Love is not always fun, but it is necessary.

4. Obedience to God.

> The way children are taught to respond to their parents is usually the way they will respond to God. Make sure that you communicate that your discipline is teaching them what God wants them to learn and not some arbitrary self-imposed standard. Also be a good example of obeying God yourself...whether you feel

like it or not. Your example is the best
teacher for how the child should respond.

Godly discipline is NOT an outlet for revenge to make
the child pay for his actions. Revenge (or punishment) is
rooted in anger and produces bitterness. Discipline is
rooted in love and produces respect and cheerful
obedience. They are very different in their purposes and
their results. One of the primary reasons parents punish
out of anger instead of discipline out of love is because
they value their own reputation more than the child's
welfare when the child misbehaves in front of other
people. Another reason is because the child's misbehavior
is inconvenient to the parent--the parent thinks he/she
has a right to a clean, quiet uninterrupted environment
and the child has violated that right. Both of these
reasons for punishment are based on selfishness, seeking
our own welfare and reputation over the welfare of the
child.

The Scriptures contain many encouraging statements
about the results of discipline. Some of these include:

- It communicates love to the child.
    Proverbs 3:12, 3:24
- It teaches wisdom and understanding.
    Proverbs 9:9, 29:15
- It teaches a proper lifestyle.
    Proverbs 6:23

- It helps overcome foolishness in a child.
  Proverbs 22:15
- It protects the child from destruction.
  Proverbs 23:12-14

> *...the consequences
> of not disciplining
> a child properly
> are bleak and
> foreboding.*

But the consequences of not disciplining a child properly are bleak and foreboding. Some of these include:

- The child will be foolish (and continue to be foolish as an adult). Proverbs 9:9

- He will experience destruction because he was not properly warned about the dangers of his misbehavior.
  Proverbs 23:12

- He develops the habit of disobedience.
  I Samuel 3:13, Ecclesiastes 8:11

- He brings shame on his parents.
  Proverbs 29:15

Discipline is a necessary teaching vehicle for the parent, but it is not the only one. The other primary method by which we teach our children is by the example we give them in our own behavior. For this reason, before getting into the discipline system you should understand how your attitudes and behavior teach values and lifestyle to your child--whether you want them to or not!

Mothers, do not expect your children to be any more cooperative within the family than you are. If you are always undermining the authority of your husband, don't be surprised when your children do not respect your authority or his.

If you habitually complain when you don't get what you want, you shouldn't wonder why your children whine and grumble when they don't get their way. Some whining usually occurs in certain stages of growing up, but if children whine consistently, it may reflect the negative attitude of one or both parents.

Many fathers value their social status or business success more highly than the development of their children.

Fathers, do not expect your children to have any more respect for governmental authority than you do. If you blatantly break the laws of the state or federal government--if you cheat on your income taxes and brag about it--then don't expect your children to be any more respectful.

Most parents would like their children to be sensitive to the needs of others. But it is naive to expect that we can be absorbed in our own interests, insensitive to what is happening in the lives of our children, and have them, especially our male children, develop compassion and sensitivity.

Many fathers value their social status or business success more highly than the development of their children. When they decide to spend a few minutes with the children, they come in like the Lone Ranger, spend a few minutes doing their fatherly duty, and then ride out into the sunset to do something "more important." Sadly, these fathers don't realize that success, status, money, boats, or even the love of their mother will not substitute for the deep need a child has for plenty of time with a loving father.

We must understand that we teach our children our value system every day. There have been many people who have come to me with their children, desiring for them to be led into a deep Christian walk, and yet they themselves have had no interest in following Christ. This is the type of person who would demand church attendance from a child when they themselves see no need to go. In most cases, your children will not have any greater value for Christ than you do.

We also teach our children how to deal with problems and pressures. Some people realistically evaluate their problems and approach them with a plan of action. Others, however, are immobilized by fear, and still others try to deny that the problem exists at all. One of the most important things we can teach our children is that God is our loving and powerful source of wisdom and strength. Do you go to God for answers? Does God have anything to do with the problems you face in life? How you deal with the rough spots will influence how your children handle them now, as well as when they are older.

A father came to me concerned about his son's displays of temper. He admitted that he had a short temper himself. What else should this man expect? He had taught his child how to deal with pressures in that way.

Discipline is a necessary tool for teaching our children to be prepared for the world...

Finally, we will teach our children how to respond to those whom we perceive to be creating problems for us. We often look for someone else to blame when something goes wrong, then we treat that person very poorly as he becomes the scapegoat for the difficulties we are experiencing.

Check out these points in your own life: Mothers, how cooperative are you? Fathers, how submissive to governmental authority are you? How sensitive are you to the needs of other people? What value systems are you teaching your children, especially how important is your Christian faith and your walk with Christ? Do you desire the same for your children? How do you deal with problems, and how do you respond to others who seem to be creating problems for you? Do you desire your children to respond in this way?

Discipline is a necessary tool for teaching our children to be prepared for the world, but it will not be very effective unless the parents model the cheerfulness, godliness, and obedience they are trying to produce in their children.

Notes:

_____
_____
_____
_____
_____
_____
_____
_____
_____
_____
_____
_____
_____
_____
_____
_____
_____

ERRORS IN DISCIPLINE

Before we examine the fundamental principles of discipline, we need to take a look at four common errors to avoid:

ANGER

Many parents get angry when their children disobey, and they respond too harshly in disciplining the child. The outburst is harmful to the child (he or she feels rejected) and harmful to the parent as well (he or she feels ashamed). Why do we respond this way? What can be done to prevent outbursts of anger when our children disobey?

Many parents try to manipulate their children through how their children's actions have made them feel.

The answer to these questions begins in a proper understanding of God's discipline of us. Hebrews 12:6 says, "Those whom the Lord loves he disciplines." His discipline, then, is not in anger. It is rooted in His love for us. Paul gives us another glimpse of the heart of God in Ephesians 4:30, which says that God is grieved when we sin. That is God's attitude toward us when we disobey Him: He is grieved because our sin is harmful to us and it dishonors Him. And this is our example for how we should discipline our children. The appropriate statement to our children is not, "You did it again, you little brat!" but rather, "It's sad that you disobeyed. I love you so much that I need to discipline you so you won't do it again." There is a world of difference between anger and grief as the motive for discipline. However, while we are expressing that their disobedience is sad, we should not focus on our sadness to make the child feel guilty for our being sad but the sadness of their destructive disobedience. I cannot overemphasize this distinction enough. Many parents try to manipulate their children through how their children's actions "have made them feel." These parents are exhibiting destructive self-centeredness. But why do we get angry when our children disobey? There may be many reasons; here are a few:

• We demand control of life because we feel we have the "right" to peace and cooperation. When children disobey, they have violated the "rights" we think we deserve.

• We may have had poor models of discipline as we grew up. Our own parents may have been quick-tempered, or maybe they repressed their anger until it was uncontrollable and became violent. Overcoming this poor example may be difficult, but it is possible by allowing God to transform our responses through diligent study of the loving discipline of God.

• We may be tired and unable to cope with the pressures of parenthood. This, however, is not a cop-out. If this reason is a frequent cause of irritibility, we need to change our interests and values so we can focus our emotional resources on our highest priorities.

• We may lack patience and get frustrated and angry if our children continue to disobey. Some children are very responsive to discipline, but some seem to need more persistence than others. That need for persistence, however, is not a threat if we recognize our security in Christ. Then we can discipline the child in love and grief if it takes one time or a hundred times to get the point across.

So then, to transform our response to our children from anger to loving grief, we need to understand the way God disciplines us so we will begin to discipline our children with the same motives God has toward us. But also, we may need to change our values and schedules so we don't get too tired to respond properly to our children.

ONE-SHOT DISCIPLINE

We would like to think that by disciplining the child one good time, we could create an environment in which the child would never perform that behavior again. But this is not realistic.

Discipline that is too severe will create resentment in the child. The discipline should represent one specific and current act, and its severity should match the severity of the offense. It should not be retroactive for accumulated mistakes and failures. Many parents, however, seem to take all the problems, mistakes and rebellious acts the child has done over a prolonged period of time and discipline him with severity so as to prevent any recurrence of those actions. If resentment is created in the child because of too severe discipline, he will rebel or create difficulties for the parent in some way. The young girl's pregnancy and the boy's stealing may be more acts of resentment than anything else.

Since many parents know nothing about disciplining with any kind of planned action they do not discipline at all, or with great severity. This is where many who are active in trying to prevent child abuse go wrong. The child abuser usually reverts back to the only kind of discipline he knows in the pressure of the situation. He goes from being permissive to cruelly punishing that which he has been allowing.

One-shot discipline often turns into punishment. There is a difference between discipline and punishment.

Punishment is used in order to inflict some kind of pain to get even because of a certain type of activity, whereas discipline is a teaching vehicle used to show the child that if he continues the undesirable behavior it will create much greater harm and pain in the future. Punishment creates great problems in the relationship between the parent and the child. We are not called to punish our children but to discipline them in a proper manner.

VERBAL DISCIPLINE

Scolding a child is designed to create emotional pain. It obviously does not cause physical pain, but creates emotional pain of the most destructive type which is not corrective, but negative.

Verbal discipline also creates a negative self-image, thereby insuring that the undesirable behavior will be repeated. If I tell Johnny, "You're a liar; you're no good; you're never going to amount to anything" and Johnny believes me, I begin to create emotional pain because I have instilled in him a sense of failure and shame. However, when this happens, the negative self-image is reinforced, for as Proverbs 23:7 tells us "...as he thinketh in his heart, so is he." And as a person sees himself, so he will act.

Verbal discipline is the primary tool used by parents today, and yet it only creates more problems for them as well as for the child.

This type of discipline also creates competition between parent and child. If the child experiences this emotional pain and domination by the parent, he will then become competitive with the parent. We misunderstand parenting if we think that it means dominating our children. The Bible speaks of teaching them but not making them simply an extension of our wills. If the child is dominated, he will in some way inflict pain upon the parent. This may not be in the form of an overt confrontation, but may involve doing poorly in school, being a troublemaker, being chronically sick, etc. This does not necessarily mean that the child is consciously determining ways to punish the parent, but if verbal discipline is severe, the parent will reap what he or she has sown.

Incidentally, you can also help your child as far as your verbalizations are concerned. Your child will not only believe your negative comments, he will also believe positive encouragements. You may say that the kid doesn't do anything right. Wrong!!! The child could not exist and not do something right. Find actions to encourage and build up your child.

One of the most common reports I hear from adults is that they don't believe they ever pleased their parents. Think about it! If you can't please your parents, who can you please? The best emotional insurance you can give your children is to let them know they are a success in your eyes.

We have seen that verbal discipline (1) creates

emotional pain, (2) forms a negative self image, insuring repetition of the undesired acts, and (3) causes competition between parent and child.

DISAGREEMENT BETWEEN PARENTS

When the mother and father of a child are not in agreement over the discipline, the child becomes part of the parents' competitiveness.

In dealing with families, I have discovered that people are either competitive or cooperative in their marriage. There are few marriages that are totally cooperative, but there are many, perhaps even a majority, that demonstrate open and sometimes hostile competition between the spouses over who is going to be in control.

The unfortunate consequence of this in the area of discipline is that the child becomes part of this competition. This pulls the child in separate directions as he tries to please both of them, and he may give up trying and go off on some destructive binge. This rebellion is primarily to draw the parents' hostility off each other and onto himself, since they have to quit fighting long enough to cooperate in trying to solve his problem. Often during divorce the child will blame himself for the situation, especially the younger child.

As a result the child sees himself as part of the problem between his parents, and he may feel he is to blame for their problems because of his misbehavior.

This creates insecurity and a great deal of guilt, especially as the competition between the spouses heightens. Or the child, in response to guilt, becomes extremely hostile towards both parents. It is not uncommon for single parents to face much rebellion in the child after the divorce.

Another unwanted consequence of disagreement between parents is the creation of erratic limits. This confuses the child and takes away his sense of security. Gross unfairness may cause resentment and then some form of rebellion later in life. As noted previously, the child may not openly confront the authority of the parent, but take his toll through some other method, including self-destructive behavior. He may get into drugs, begin to have "emotional problems" that could last for the rest of his life. This leaves the parents with the feeling of having failed, which is exactly what the child is trying to do.

So there are three things that may occur when there is disagreement between parents. (1) The child may become part of the parents' competition. (2) He may internalize the parents' problem as his fault and put a great deal of guilt upon himself. (3) The disagreement may create erratic limits of discipline and promote resentment and self-destructive rebellion.

The dangers of incorrect discipline are many, and certainly any parent would want to avoid these errors. As with every aspect of life, the Bible gives us the guidelines we need to discipline in the proper manner.

The dangers of incorrect discipline are many, and certainly any parent would want to avoid these errors.

Notes:

_____
_____
_____
_____
_____
_____
_____
_____
_____
_____
_____
_____
_____
_____
_____
_____
_____
_____
_____
_____
_____
_____
_____
_____
_____
_____

EXAMPLES OF DISCIPLINE

The best, and indeed the only way to avoid the errors in discipline is to follow the example set for us by our heavenly Father as He disciplines his children. We need to understand six details concerning His method before we apply it to our actions:

> 1. *The Father does not violate our will.* There is a school of thought that says "Break their will but not their spirit." I believe that should be revised to say, "Teach them to use their will correctly." We desire not to break or dominate the will of our children, but to teach them that there are certain consequences to making poor choices. If we simply break their will, we set up a situation that later in life will create tremendous difficulty toward making correct choices. The Father does not force us to choose that which is right for us. He does let us experience the results of erroneous decisions.

2. _The Father does limit some choices_ which we may or may not make. (He says that He does not permit us to be tempted past that which we can stand, but gives us a way of escape. I Corinthians 10:13) When our children are small, they are not capable of controlling their will effectively; therefore, instead of allowing them to have total freedom, we must limit their mobility in order to limit the choices they have to make.

For instance, the child may be playing in the front yard and run into the street to retrieve a ball. One of our rules would be that he never go into the street, and when that occurs the first time, we should discipline him. The second time he does this in spite of the discipline, and because of the danger involved, we may remove him from the front yard altogether until he demonstrates he is making better choices, being more obedient in other areas.

3. Although He does convict us of sin, _the Father does not verbally shame us._ For those of us who are His children, His workmanship, His new creations, He does not desire for us to be ashamed of our person.

He wants us to recognize the destructiveness of sin. We need to be able to confess our sin without failing to recognize Christ's finished work in us.

If you look at the introductions Paul gives in many of his epistles, you will find that even though he may be about to discuss with them some undesired activities of the church, he still addresses them as "saints." In Colossians 3, for example, he calls the church members "elect of God, holy, and beloved," where earlier in the chapter he referred to their immoral and impure activities.

That is the way the Father relates to us. He has taken care of our sin and has made us absolutely righteous and innocent, as if we'd never sinned before (Romans 5:1). We are justified, and there is no place in Scripture where you find God placing guilt or verbally shaming the believer.

4. *The Father teaches us what is profitable and unprofitable.* He desires for us to understand that sin is destructive. The problem with most of us is that we are not convinced that sin is destructive. (Many times we base our activity on how guilty we feel while we are doing it or how bad we felt after we did it the last time.)

I have seen people do some of the most hurtful, ugly acts and because they don't feel guilty, they judge it must not be all that bad. This seems especially true with sexual sins.

Sometimes it takes many laps around the

course of life before we become convinced that what the Bible calls sin is destructive. However, rest assured; your Father is a tireless teacher and is going to teach us this fact.

5. The Father teaches us that sin is unprofitable by the principle that we reap what we sow. The Father warns that He is not mocked, but that we can be assured that we will reap that which we sow (Galatians 6:7).

6. God disciplines His children out of love. Psalm 32 speaks of the heavy hand of God. This not only speaks of God's decisive manner but also His consistency as the Father describes himself in I Corinthians 4:8. He says that He is love and we can be assured that His love will influence and guide His discipline.

After studying I Corinthians 13:4-8 answer the following questions:

A. Although powerful, God is patient and bears ill treatment. Do you?

B. The Father is kind and gentle to the point of softening that which is harsh. Are you?

C. He does not envy anything His children might have. Do you?

D. The Father does not try to put His children down by bragging or showing off how great He is. Do you?

E. The Father does not allow HImself to be exasperated or aroused to uncontrollable anger. Do you?

F. The Father does not keep long lists of past failures to hold over our heads. Do you?

G. He does not rejoice in His children's failures. Do you?

H. The Father bears up under all things without losing heart or courage. Do you?

At this point you may be saying you are just human and cannot do all those things. This simply points up our need to resist trying to use our human strength and to rely on Christ.

Notes:

_____
_____
_____
_____
_____
_____

WHAT TYPE OF DISCIPLINE
IS APPROPRIATE?

How do you determine which kind of discipline is appropriate in a given situation? Here are some common sense principles to help you decide what will be the most helpful way of communicating strong, loving discipline:

> 1. Seek God's guidance. The training of our children is one of the most important priorities in our lives. It is often a difficult task, and we need the Lord's help. Read the passages in Proverbs, Ephesians 6:1-4, and other pertinent passages to get God's wisdom. Then pray for His guidance as you make plans for teaching and warning your children through discipline.

> 2. Know your child. The responsiveness and maturity of children varies not only as they grow older, but also within an age group. Therefore, you need to know how each of your children individually responds to discipline.

Often siblings are of such differing personalities that a different type of discipline is needed for each one at any given age. For some sensitive and responsive children, spankings are seldom necessary, while other children seem to need persistent corporal discipline to get a point across.

3. Avoid revenge. The purposes of discipline are warning and teaching the child, not punishing the child. Our response should be firm but kind. If you find yourself in an attitude of revenge, do not spank the child. Corporal punishment from this attitude will damage the child's self-esteem as well as the parent's relationship with the child. Take time to cool down emotionally, then talk lovingly, calmly, and firmly with the child about his behavior. If too much time has not passed corporal discipline may still be in order.

The responsiveness and maturity of children varies not only as they grow older, but also within an age group.

4. Be selective. There are three major options

for discipline, and the selection of the appropriate one depends on the situation. These are:

• *Logical consequence.* Many times there is a logical consequence to disobedience. If you tell a child to be home for supper by 6:00 p.m. and he comes home at 6:30 p.m., the consequence of not have a valid excuse may be that he doesn't get to eat supper.

In another common occurrence, if a child isn't doing well in school, it may be the logical consequence of not spending time studying. Spanking may not be nearly as helpful as requiring the child to spend an increasing amount of time studying each day until the grades are acceptable.

• *Withdrawal of privilege.* The withdrawal of some privilege may communicate more clearly than corporal discipline as the child grows older. (This booklet contains a section that shows how to select the privilege to be withheld.)

• *Corporal discipline.* This type of discipline should be used for obvious rebellion against authority. The spanking should not be administered by a person's hand because the hand is supposed to communicate love and affection.

Proverbs 13:24 says to use a rod--a thin flexible stick or switch which causes some pain but does not injure the child. The spanking should consist of three or four swats given on the rear or back of the legs, never on the hands. The bones, tendons, and nerves in the hand are much too tender.

Be careful not to use physical discipline for any and every situation. If the child was told something and then has forgotten, he needs to be reminded, not spanked. (Here, of course, you need to know your child and determine if he has truly forgotten.) Also, it is improper to give the child two glasses of Kool-Aid and three Twinkies and then spank the child for unruly behavior. A "sugar high" is not the child's fault. Try to get the child to a tranquil environment until he calms down, and don't give the child such quantities of sugar anymore.

Spanking can be used to teach the child when he begins to learn from external sources. This may be relatively early for some children, but not until one and a half years for others. Spanking should be stopped as the child grows up when it become humiliating or when it provokes anger instead of sorrow.

As children grow and mature, the selection of the type of discipline will change accordingly. When children are small, spanking and withdrawal of privileges are effective. But as they mature, spanking should be used more and more sparingly until it is no longer used at all. Instead, the logical consequences of the child's actions and withdrawal of privileges will be increasingly effective in developing a person who is mature and responsible.

Notes:

_____

_____

_____

_____

_____

_____

_____

_____

_____

_____

_____

_____

_____

_____

_____

_____

_____

_____

_____

_____

THE DISCIPLINE SYSTEM

With all the preceding information as a background, let us look at a system designed to be consistent with the Father's discipline. The system itself is based on four lists, which do not take a great deal of time, but require some observation of your child. If you are willing to put forth this effort you can set up a system which will aid you in disciplining your children.

>   1. Make a list of how your child spends his or her free time. Many parents make the mistake of using for discipline that which is unimportant to the child. For instance, sending a child to his room when he wants to be in his room anyway is not really discipline. For us to be able to have some leverage, and to create some understanding of the seriousness of the act the child has performed, we must determine what is important to him.

Include some chores the child would not desire to do, but would be required of him after breaking a rule. This could be washing windows or pulling weeds, chores that would not necessarily have to be done in the maintenance of the home, but would be nice to have done. Here is an example of such a list (please see #1 under the Work-Section in the back of the booklet to make your own list):

1. Playing with neighbors' children
2. Watching TV
3. Riding bike
4. Allowance
5. Going swimming
6. Putting models together
7. Spending the night
8. Stereo listening
9. Lawn weeding
10. Window washing
11. Washing the car

2. Include what you have written in the first line, put in order the priority, beginning with that which is most important down to that which is least important to the child. This list of priorities might read as follows (please see #2 under the Work-Section in the back of the booklet to make your own list):

1. Watching TV
2. Playing with neighbors' children
3. Receiving allowance
4. Going swimming
5. Riding bike
6. Spending the night
7. Weeding the front lawn - 3 hours
8. Putting models together
9. Stereo listening
10. Washing windows
11. Washing the car

You cannot successfully discipline a bad attitude, but you can discipline your child when he talks back, glares...

---

3. Take numbers six, five, and four from the second list and put them at the top of the third list. The list now reads six, five, four, one, two, three, seven, eight, nine, ten, eleven.

Notice what has been done. You have decided generally what is important to the child. You put these in an order of priority. Finally, you put three others which are not the most important to the top of the list. This is done so that the

---

child will know you are going to be consistent without always taking away the most important activity from him while he learns.

The next step is to set forth the limits (please see #3 under the Work-Section in the back of the booklet to make your own list):

- WHAT is going to be disciplined

- WHY it is going to be disciplined

- HOW it is going to be disciplined

The "what" must be something that can be observed. You cannot successfully discipline a bad attitude, but you can discipline your child when he talks back, glares, mumbles, and for other outward expressions. If you can't describe a behavior, you can't discipline it, but those activities that will cause problems for the child in the future should be included. For example, if the child is chronically late, when he gets out of the home and into a job, he will find that the world is much less tolerant of laziness and non-punctuality than his parents. He may lose jobs, he may go through financial problems, he may even lose friends due to being late to social engagements. Therefore, punctuality would be something that you would want to discipline.

Confronting authority by "talking back" is another area

you would want to discipline because out in the world the boss will not keep an employee who is abusive when something does not go his way, or when he is given a job he does not want to do. That which is to be disciplined is that which will harm the child. Then, you must have a good reason WHY you are going to demand certain limits on behavior. If you cannot come up with a reason for the limitation, you probably have something that is an irritant to you, but is not necessarily something the child needs to cease doing.

For instance, a child may make a mess while taking something apart. After he is through playing and puts everything away, it may bother you that he is not neat. Yet, in order to allow the child the freedom to explain the world around him, you must tolerate his occasionally being messy or dirty.

Now we determine HOW the discipline is going to be administered. In order to do so, we must understand that there are three types of discipline:

> 1. Natural Discipline. You tell a child not to touch the stove because it is hot. He does touch it and burns himself. It is not necessary to discipline the child further because he is hurting already.

> 2. Logical Discipline. If the child is told to be home by a certain time for dinner and he is late, he misses out on eating. He was late, therefore

the logical answer is that he misses the activity.

3. Purposeful Discipline. This occurs when the child loses something off his list, and perhaps includes spanking which is an acceptable form of discipline, especially during the pre-teenage years. It does have a limited time of effect, however, since once the child is spanked, the event then becomes past history. There is seldom any occasion in our lives that we get ourselves in trouble and then have the effects of the trouble over as quickly as a simple spanking. I do believe that spanking should

---

...spanking should be used when the child is confronting authority or is doing something wrong in a planned, plotted out way.

---

be used particularly when the child is confronting authority or is doing something wrong in a planned, plotted out way. On these occasions it is appropriate to spank the child and also have him lose something off his list to extend the time of discipline. This would represent what would happen to him in a real life situation if he were to violate certain rules. We are simply getting the child ready for life.

The length of time a child should lose a certain object or activity is important. The younger the child, the less time you have to take any one thing away from him. You want him to experience the loss of something important to him, but not so long that he ceases to look forward to doing it. If this occurs, you lose that activity or object as a tool of discipline. For instance, if you take a child's bike away for a month, his life patterns will change so much that the bike will no longer be important. It would make a greater impact for him to lose his bike five times in a month than to lose it only once. It is not necessarily the severity of the discipline as is the repeated sense of loss that makes the difference.

For a toddler, you can use "time out" plus spanking. Time out is a mechanism during which the child is stopped from whatever activity he is doing and kept quiet for a few minutes. When he begins to have a set pattern of behavior or activities that he looks forward to, then you can begin to develop your list to take advantage of those important activities. You must remember that to a very young child, what appears to be a reasonably short period of time to you may seem almost like an eternity to him. For a young child to lose something for several weeks is almost

incomprehensible. If it is taken away for too
long, the child loses any hope of gaining it back.
　By this time, your fourth list has been compiled as
follows:

　　　1. What is to be disciplined.
　　　2. Why it is to be disciplined.
　　　3. How the discipline is to be administered,
　　　including length of discipline time (lists one,
　　　two and three).

　After you have developed your list of things that you
are going to take away and your list of limits, write this
statement: *"Before God we commit ourselves to
performing in the discipline system."* Below that, you and
your spouse sign your names. Notice you have not asked
your child to sign his name because it is not up to him to
discipline himself.
　Underneath your names write, *"I understand the above
limits"* and have the child write his name to show that he
is aware of what is going to be done. You are not asking
the child to lie by making a promise to keep all the rules;
you simply have him indicate that he understands. You
then give him a copy of the limits and the items that will
be taken away.
　In the case of children who do not read, you will have
to sit down daily with them for a couple of weeks and
help them memorize the list. Even very small children
find it easy to memorize. Incidentally, when you have to

refer to the list for something to take away, you take the highest item on the list. You may be down to number eight, but if number two has just become available, you take away number two.

With this plan there are no surprises. The child knows just what to expect and where his limits are. This, coupled with consistency by the parents, goes a long way toward building a sense of security in a child.

Notes:_____

_____
_____
_____
_____
_____
_____
_____
_____
_____
_____
_____
_____
_____
_____
_____
_____
_____
_____

QUESTIONS ABOUT DISCIPLINING

Whenever I present this plan to parents, inevitably there are questions. I feel it would be helpful to cover some typical ones I have received.

1. *How many licks do I give the child?*

The Bible speaks of using a rod which means a flexible stick or switch. A very thin switch will not cause harm, yet the sting is sufficient. I have also found it useful to call this switch the rod of discipline. And I would rarely, if ever, suggest that a child receive over three licks for anything. In fact, two are usually enough. Remember, you are not trying to make it one-shot discipline.

I have heard people say that we should keep spanking a child until he cried. This is a poor understanding of children. He will either cry very easily to manipulate you, or, because he feels he is being interpersonally dominated, will refuse to give you the "satisfaction" of seeing him cry. In one case, you teach the child to manipulate and in the other you reinforce bitterness. Remember, you are not trying to break the child's will but to teach him to use it wisely.

Your consistency of discipline will have a much greater effect on the child's behavior than the number of licks given or the fact that he was made to cry.

2. *I've tried this before. Is my child different?*

There is one of two things wrong with your system. Either you have not developed a list of what is really important to the child, or you may just be inconsistent. I have never seen this system fail when the list represents what is important to the child and when the parents are consistent.

...you are not trying to break the child's will but to teach him to use it wisely.

---

3. *Are there any universal rules?*

Yes, there are a couple that I think should always be on the list. First, the child is always disciplined for confronting and talking back to authority. This is not tolerated outside the home, and should not be in the home. At the same time we do not want to teach the child to be passive and never speak up when wronged. However, there is a right and wrong way of "speaking up." The child may not confront the parent with aggressive verbalization nor may he, as one of my client's children did, walk down the hall mumbling. He mumbled loud enough for the parents to hear, and I told that parent to explain to the child that audible mumbling was considered the same as rebuking openly. You should give the child an opportunity to explain in a manner which you recognize would be tolerated outside the home.

4. *What if the child feels I am unfair?*

One of the most beneficial things you can teach your child is that life is unfair. You don't attempt to be unfair in your dealings with him, but he must learn to relate to authority when he feels that authority is being unfair. Again, if the child has some grievance to communicate, he must learn to do it in a manner which would be acceptable outside the home. For instance, if you are too busy to discuss the matter right then, or if you think the child is simply trying to be argumentative, you might require him to make an appointment with you in order to discuss this grievance. It is not to be discussed after the discipline is set. You should make your appointment with your child not during some time in which you have a lot of things to do, but perhaps when the child has something that he is doing. It would not be unreasonable for you to make the appointment during a favorite television program of the child. This will test whether the child really has something legitimate or not. If he wants to discuss a matter, he will take the time out of his schedule. If the discipline includes spanking, you simply delay the spanking until you have had your discussion. During any discussions, if you are wrong, please admit it.

Second, the parent must not nag the child. You will give him a great payoff when you cease nagging. But what happens when the child does not seem to hear you? If that happens, for the next week require the child to come and stand before you and repeat back to you what you have asked him to do. You will find that sometimes we teach our children to be deaf because we allow them to get away with not hearing. You cannot tell whether the child has been ignoring you or not, but at least he will begin to be more sensitive to what you are saying if he is required to come and stand before you to receive his instructions. You should have as a goal to tell the child his instructions one at a time.

Incidentally, you do not try to motivate the child to live within the limits prior to his breaking them. For example, if you have as one of your rules that the bed should be made by 7:30 in the morning and you see it unmade at 7:25, you say nothing to the child. He must learn how to make his decision, how to plan, in order to meet the rules he will find in this world. You wait until 7:30 and then inform the child that he has violated on his limits. You are not there to remind him of the limits after he knows what they are. One of the most pathetic people I have ever seen was a young woman in her twenties who could not make any decisions without her mother telling her what to do.

5. *What if my child refuses to accept this system?*

This is a common question of parents with teenagers, and is not an unlikely occurrence. Children today have a great deal more mobility and if they desire not to do something, they can elude their parents. Many parents are totally out of control in situations with their teenagers. They state that they love their children but just do not know how in the world they are going to get them under control.

If your child refuses to place himself under the discipline program, and therefore under your authority, you must adopt a policy of "tough love" in your home. "Tough love" can be brought about in many ways, one of which is to apply enough pressure on your child to bring his behavior under control. It would not be uncommon, for example, for me to recommend to parents that they escort their child to literally every function they are involved in. This will often work to combat the primary motivation of every child and adolescent-peer pressure. If this fails, it will then be necessary for you to obtain professional help in order to intervene in the life of your child, which may lead to obtaining help from a Christ-centered treatment program such as Rapha.

If your teenager is out of control and, as parents, you do not apply the pressure necessary to control his behavior, you are in a very real sense contributing to his destruction. Taking steps to control your child's behavior lets him know how very much you love him and care about his future.

If you simply sit there and allow the child to do his thing, you may think that you are doing it out of a sense of love and devotion, but I have my doubts about that. I believe you may be doing it out of a sense of guilt instead, trying to make up for something or as an attempt to win popularity with the child.

6. *My child is too young.*

I hear this from those with two and three year olds. I had some dear friends with a little girl of about 16 months who was into everything. Her parents had read books that said that a young child could not be disciplined, but out of desperation one day the young mother spanked the little girl. To her amazement, the child neither broke nor was emotionally crushed. In fact, she started avoiding that for which she was spanked. My comment to those parent with two and three year olds is that if you can teach an earthworm to do tricks (and you can), you can control your child.

7. *Doesn't spanking create aggression and child abuse?*

Child abuse occurs when discipline is erratic. If there is no systematic method of discipline, abuse generally occurs. If the abuse is not physical, it will be verbal. Verbal abuse is the most prevalent form of abuse and may be the most destructive. It is true that physical discipline can be easily abused yet God instructed us to use it as long as it is discipline and not punishment (God did not instruct us to haul off and hit our kids when we get mad at them and then blame it on Him). If you get any pleasure out of using the rod of discipline don't use it until you deal with yourself.

As far as teaching your child to be aggressive, you really need not worry that your discipline is going to play a part in that as long as it is administered in love and consistency. He will learn aggressiveness from sources other than your discipline.

...if you can teach an earthworm to do tricks (and you can), you can get control over your child.

8. *How can I be sure this system works?*

If you use the system in its entirety, without skipping any steps or doing anything other than what is set down here, it will work. I have never seen it fail when used consistently, and I have seen it used with children who are very disturbed emotionally, as well as with normal children. There are two major benefits of this system. First, it takes the child out of competition with the parent. He does not have the ability to manipulate the parents because the system is written down in black and white. (Your system will be ten times weaker if you do not put it all down on paper.) Verbal systems are always weaker.

Second, it improves the parent-child relationship because (1) the child is no longer in a struggle with the parent and (2) he is relaxed in knowing that his parent is providing the security he needs.

One of the most frightening things for a young child is to realize that he has manipulative power over his parents. In fact, many times later in life, in talking to these children, I hear them express a great deal of hatred toward their parents. They felt no security because they could do whatever they wanted to do. The parents have attempted to be pleasing and win a popularity contest with their children, and are shocked to find that their children want little to do with them because of the insecurity they felt when growing up.

You can bring peace into your home and great benefits to your children by using this simple system.

WORK-SECTION

This section is provided for family use to evaluate and record priorities, losses and disciplines.

1. How my child spends his/her free time.
(See page 38)

Name of Child _____

      1. _____
      2. _____
      3. _____
      4. _____
      5. _____
      6. _____
      7. _____
      8. _____
      9. _____
    10. _____
    11. _____
    12. _____
    13. _____
    14. _____
    15. _____
    16. _____

Name of Child _____

1. _____
2. _____
3. _____
4. _____
5. _____
6. _____
7. _____
8. _____
9. _____
10. _____
11. _____
12. _____
13. _____
14. _____
15. _____
16. _____

Name of Child _____

1. _____
2. _____
3. _____
4. _____
5. _____
6. _____
7. _____
8. _____
9. _____
10. _____
11. _____
12. _____
13. _____
14. _____
15. _____
16. _____

Name of Child _____

1. _____
2. _____
3. _____
4. _____
5. _____
6. _____
7. _____
8. _____
9. _____
10. _____
11. _____
12. _____
13. _____
14. _____
15. _____
16. _____

2. Child's priorities listing from most important to least important. (See pages 38 and 39)

Name of Child _____

1. _____
2. _____
3. _____
4. _____
5. _____
6. _____
7. _____
8. _____
9. _____
10. _____
11. _____
12. _____
13. _____
14. _____
15. _____
16. _____

Name of Child

1. _____
2. _____
3. _____
4. _____
5. _____
6. _____
7. _____
8. _____
9. _____
10. _____
11. _____
12. _____
13. _____
14. _____
15. _____
16. _____

Name of Child _____

1. _____
2. _____
3. _____
4. _____
5. _____
6. _____
7. _____
8. _____
9. _____
10. _____
11. _____
12. _____
13. _____
14. _____
15. _____
16. _____

Name of Child _____

    1. _____

    2. _____

    3. _____

    4. _____

    5. _____

    6. _____

    7. _____

    8. _____

    9. _____

  10. _____

  11. _____

  12. _____

  13. _____

  14. _____

  15. _____

  16. _____

3. Revised priority list to establish an appropriate listing of potential "losses" for the child. (See page 40)

Child's Name _____

ACTIVITY   **FOR WHAT DURATION**

1. _____   _____
2. _____   _____
3. _____   _____
4. _____   _____
5. _____   _____
6. _____   _____
7. _____   _____
8. _____   _____
9. _____   _____
10. _____   _____
11. _____   _____
12. _____   _____
13. _____   _____
14. _____   _____

Child's Name _____

ACTIVITY   FOR WHAT DURATION

1. _____   _____

2. _____   _____

3. _____   _____

4. _____   _____

5. _____   _____

6. _____   _____

7. _____   _____

8. _____   _____

9. _____   _____

10. _____   _____

11. _____   _____

12. _____   _____

13. _____   _____

14. _____   _____

Child's Name _____

ACTIVITY   **FOR WHAT DURATION**

1. _____   _____

2. _____   _____

3. _____   _____

4. _____   _____

5. _____   _____

6. _____   _____

7. _____   _____

8. _____   _____

9. _____   _____

10. _____   _____

11. _____   _____

12. _____   _____

13. _____   _____

14. _____   _____

Child's Name _____

ACTIVITY   **FOR WHAT DURATION**

1. _____   _____
2. _____   _____
3. _____   _____
4. _____   _____
5. _____   _____
6. _____   _____
7. _____   _____
8. _____   _____
9. _____   _____
10. _____   _____
11. _____   _____
12. _____   _____
13. _____   _____
14. _____   _____

Setting the limits !

EXAMPLE:

1. What is disciplined?

Not straightening room by 7:30

2. Why it is disciplined?

To teach personal responsibility

3. How is it going to be disciplined?

Lose highest item on Revised List #3

Child's Name _____

1. What?_____

2. Why?_____

3. How?_____

Child's Name _____

1. What?_____

2. Why?_____

3. How?_____

Child's Name _____

1. What?_____

2. Why?_____

3. How?_____

Child's Name _____

1. What?_____

2. Why?_____

3. How?_____

Child's Name _____

1. What?_____

2. Why?_____

3. How?_____

Child's Name _____

1. What?_____

2. Why?_____

3. How?_____

Child's Name _____

1. What?_____

2. Why?_____

3. How?_____

Child's Name _____

1. What?_____

2. Why?_____

3. How?_____

Child's Name _____

1. What?_____

2. Why?_____

3. How?_____

Child's Name _____

1. What?_____

2. Why?_____

3. How?_____

Child's Name _____

1. What?_____

2. Why?_____

3. How?_____

Child's Name _____

1. What?_____

2. Why?_____

3. How?_____

Child's Name _____

1. What?_____

2. Why?_____

3. How?_____

Child's Name _____

1. What?_____

2. Why?_____

3. How?_____

Child/Parent Discipline Covenant

CHILD

I have read and understand the priority schedule and free time loss system that will help me to develop stronger disciplines in my life.

_____
Child's Signature

PARENTS

I commit myself to implementing this discipline system because of my love for _____ and our combined desire to character development in his/her life.

_____
Parent's Signature

_____
Parent's Signature

Child/Parent Discipline Covenant

CHILD

I have read and understand the priority schedule and free time loss system that will help me to develop stronger disciplines in my life.

_____
Child's Signature

PARENTS

I commit myself to implementing this discipline system because of my love for _____ and our combined desire to character development in his/her life.

_____
Parent's Signature

_____
Parent's Signature

Child/Parent Discipline Covenant

CHILD

I have read and understand the priority schedule and free time loss system that will help me to develop stronger disciplines in my life.

_____

Child's Signature

PARENTS

I commit myself to implementing this discipline system because of my love for _____ and our combined desire to character development in his/her life.

_____

Parent's Signature

_____

Parent's Signature

Dear Reader,

I know you are aware of the emotional, mental, and substance abuse problems that impact our Christian community today. You may be facing severe problems in your own family with drug abuse or a rebellious child. Or possibly you know someone who is in need of help.

I want to take these pages to share with you about an organization that I formed to offer a special kind of treatment. The organization is called Rapha.

When we began Rapha in early 1986, little did we know the extent of the need for, or anticipate the national response to our program of in-hospital and extensive outpatient Christ-centered therapy. Our initial perception of Rapha certainly did not envision our expansion to numerous, nationwide cities and programs.

Professional, qualified and committed therapists and program directors, who hold strongly to a Christ-centered therapy program, based on the believer's personhood in Jesus Christ, have joined us in becoming the nation's largest provider of Christ-centered therapy.

The Rapha program provides treatment for adults and adolescents for psychiatric, alcohol, chemical dependency, and eating disorder problems.

We are approved by most major insurance carriers and offer a *travel assistance program* for those who must leave their own city to be admitted to one of our hospital programs.

We have networked with many major ministries who collectively receive millions of calls annually for prayer and help. Rapha provides a nationwide referral source immediately capable of handling those calls which would generally be considered "crises," 24 hours a day.

In short, we want to be available to you. With units throughout the United States we want you to be aware of this opportunity to refer those who contact you, or your organization, with needs serious enough to require hospitalization...and refer them to a quality, Christ-centered program.

Sincerely,

Robert S. McGee
President

75

A BALANCED APPROACH
OF
CLINICAL
&
BIBLICAL

To do therapy on a Christ-centered basis, we must come to terms with certain questions.

1. Do we really believe that the Bible is the correct resource in which to find answers to our emotional problems?

2. Is the Bible a textbook for counseling?

3. Did Christ truly come to earth to give His children abundant life?

A counseling model may be called Christ-centered if it never violates what the Bible teaches about ethical standards and doctrinal issues. The Bible is the ultimate yardstick for measuring truth.

Much of secular psychology is built upon the theory that introspection and self-examination will somehow allow the patient to change and get well. But introspection can become a means of avoiding rather than assuming responsibility. While Christ-centered therapists would certainly agree that introspection can be helpful in identifying problem areas from the past, it is important to note that introspection alone does not cause people to get well. Christ-centered therapy, then, involves an uncovering of what has been deeply hidden for the purpose of promoting dependence--rather than independence--dependence on who we are as a person rather than the world's system of performance and the opinion of others.

PROGRAMS OFFERED

Rapha operates both adult and adolescent units that clearly define and educate patients about the emotional, physical and spiritual dimensions of their problems.

Rapha provides both general psychiatric and chemical dependency programs within their adolescent and adult units.

Rapha strongly confronts identity issues brought by peer and/or parental pressures, and clearly defines the need to understand "self-worth" from a perspective of Christian personhood rather than the performance demands of a world system.

Rapha's program directors, counselors, therapists and support staff meet the professional requirements of state and federal government agencies and are properly credentialed by each hospital. Program directors and therapists are Rapha employees.

Rapha units operate in JCAH-approved hospitals, with associated partial hospital units beginning in several metropolitan areas.

Rapha manages autonomous units within existing hospitals directing all phases of treatment within the structure of the hospital's by-laws.

A typical Rapha unit is completely separate from the other units in the hospital. Patients do not co-mingle with the general hospital population.

Patients and appropriate family members are transported to the nearest appropriate Rapha Unit. A travel assistance program is also available for patients and family at Rapha's expense.

Rapha is committed to providing and/or facilitating the aftercare treatment of discharged patients.

The Rapha Adult Psychiatric Program

When resolution of problems in living is not effected within the individual's ecological group or through alternatives to hospitalization, inpatient care is indicated. Hospitalization provides treatment resources of skilled mental health professionals and is directed at assisting the individual to develop self-enhancing awareness, attitudes, and behavior patterns necessary for meaningful social functioning.

The Rapha Adult Program responds to the psychiatric, spiritual, and chemical dependency needs of adults, ages 18 or older, requiring 24-hour skilled care.

The program adheres to the belief that there are strong and viable "changing agents" inherent in the Christian's basic faith. These change agents, then, are used in therapy to aid the individual in moving toward wellness, including family and community reentry. Rapha therapists have strong commitment to Christ in their daily lives, and in addition, understand the necessary interaction that takes place between the believer's emotional and spiritual dynamic. Involvement of the patient's family throughout the treatment process is considered essential. The treatment program works closely with the family to restore healthy family relationships

The Rapha Adolescent Psychiatric Program

The philosophy of the Adolescent Program responds to the psychiatric, spiritual, and chemical dependency needs of adolescents, ages 12 through 18, requiring 24-hour skilled care.

Yet another premise of the inpatient program is that problem resolution and skills development are best facilitated through the use of a highly structured therapeutic environment.

A family assessment is also conducted to determine their level of adaptive functioning.

In addition to individual and family therapies, group therapies and activities form the core of the therapeutic effort. With adolescents, this effort is focused on increasing and enhancing coping, socialization, and communication skills through role playing and verbal-cognitive oriented therapies. The effort also emphasizes developing behavioral insight and the learning of alternatives to dysfunctional behavior. Other therapies focus on the development of age-appropriate motor skills, cooperative effort, relaxation and leisure time management. In addition, the program also offers pre-vocational planning and counseling when indicated.

A comprehensive school program provides individualized educational assessment and programming through certified Special Education teachers.

The program treatment interventions focus on the reduction or elimination of the adolescent's stressful subjective experiences. Additionally, the program fosters the reduction or elimination of maladaptive behaviors to the extent that inpatient treatment is no longer indicated.

Throughout the inpatient experience, discharge and aftercare planning involving the adolescent and his/her family or guardian is an ongoing process.

Adolescents, ages 12 through 18, requiring 24-hour skilled care.

The program is based on the belief that adolescents need a secure, structured and supportive environment in which to work through developmental, psychological, social, spiritual, and familial adjustment problems. This program is designed to go beyond the traditional forms of treatment to address the spiritual dimensions of the adolescent patient.

The program adheres to the belief that there are strong and viable "changing agents" inherent in the Christian's basic faith. These change agents, then, are used in therapy to aid the individual in moving toward wellness, including family and community reentry.

Basic To All Staff

Rapha therapists have a strong commitment to Christ in their daily lives, and in addition, understand the necessary interaction that takes place between the believer's emotional and spiritual dynamic.

Yet another premise of the inpatient program is that problem resolution and skills development are best facilitated through the use of a highly structured therapeutic environment.

An active multidisciplinary treatment approach is employed by receiving input from the disciplines of psychiatry, psychology, social service, nursing, special education, occupational, recreational, and other therapies. Highly trained and competent professional hospital program therapists provide individual, group, and family psychotherapy.

Group therapies with adolescents are focused on increasing and enhancing coping, socialization, and communication skills through role playing and verbal-cognitive oriented therapies.

A comprehensive school program provides individualized educational assessment and programming through certified Special Education teachers.

Additionally, the program fosters the reduction or elimination of maladaptive behaviors to the extent that inpatient treatment is no longer indicated. Simultaneous emphases are placed on facilitating adaptive, independent functioning and problem-solving skills, strengthening self-esteem, and improving family and peer relationships within the parameters of the Christian lifestyle.

Throughout the inpatient experience, discharge and aftercare planning involving the adolescent and his/her family or guardian is an ongoing process. The aim is one of maintaining treatment gains and providing for a smooth transition to the post-hospital environment.

For Additional Information About The Rapha Treatment

Programs and the Locations of our Treatment Centers....Call

1-800-227-2657
TOLL FREE / 24-HOURS